POLITICALLY CORRECT

CORRECT

CENSORSHIP
IN AMERICAN
CULTURE

FAITH AND FREEDOM
SERIES

POLITICALLY CORRECT

CENSORSHIP IN AMERICAN CULTURE

JOHN W. WHITEHEAD

MOODY PRESS
CHICAGO

ISBN: 0-8024-6680-X

1 3 5 7 9 10 8 6 4 2

Printed in the United States of America

An alarming debate has arisen in Massachusetts regarding the appropriate content of advertisements in a high school newspaper. The controversy began when some parents in a community sought to "advertise" a message to students alongside commercial advertisements appearing in the local high school newspaper and yearbook. The parents' advertisement simply read: "We know you can do it! Abstinence: The Healthy Choice."[1]

The ten-word message promoting sexual abstinence was rejected for publication by both school officials and the high school newspaper editorial board.[2] The parents' message was deemed too "controversial," "political," and "objectionable" to appear within the pages of either the newspaper or the yearbook.[3]

It is disheartening to learn that public promotion of abstinence by parents could be termed "objectionable." Nonetheless, rejection of the advertisement might be defensible if it were part of a sincere school district effort to allow parents alone to educate their children about sexual issues. Such a policy of restraint would demonstrate respect for the sensibilities of the families that the school district serves.

However, rationalization of the advertisement's rejection based on its "controversial" nature seems disingenuous in light of other actions of this school district. For example, the same school has distributed condoms to minors from inside the high school since 1992.[4] The school supplies condoms to students without requiring parental consent, and only recently has the program been revised to include information about abstinence in the "condom packet."[5] To say the least, condom distribution in the public schools without parental consent would seem at least as "controversial" as a parental advertisement promoting abstinence.

There are many interesting aspects to the rejection of the parents' abstinence advertisement. One of the most troubling is also one of the most subtle: "political correctness."

"Controversial" or Politically Incorrect?

There is a distinction between a school's refusal to print any and/or all messages by parents in the school newspaper and a school's refusal to print an abstinence message that it deems too "controversial" in light of a school district policy of distributing condoms. The former represents an action that is ostensibly content-neutral. The latter represents an action mandated, at least in part, by political correctness. One of the hallmarks of political correctness is inconsistency in the treatment of ideas that are deemed "correct" and "incorrect."

In the abstinence ad matter, the school district created a double standard for the expression of opinions about teenage sexual activity. Although undoubtedly controversial, both the high school's "Life Skills" course and school-based condom distribution communicate that teenage sexual intercourse is natural and acceptable.[6] As an opposing view, however, the parents' advertisement was censored as "controversial."

Political Correctness: It's More than It Appears

Media and other discussions about "political correctness" ("PC") controversies often leave the impression that the effects of PC speech restrictions have been positive, or at least largely benign.[7] PC is often portrayed as a well-intentioned but sometimes misunderstood attempt to eliminate prejudice through, for example, the renaming of sports teams[8] or consciousness-raising acts of political activism.[9]

However, the example from Massachusetts illustrates another aspect of the issue. Both formally and informally, notions of political correctness inhibit the freedom to dissent from a lengthening litany of "approved" positions on matters of family, gender, and sexual orientation.

PC has designated certain ideas as "correct" and "incorrect," and works to suppress the expression of "incorrect" ideas. The consequence is that some people—most often religious people and others with a traditional moral view—are unable to speak and act according to their convictions. This too often results in religious apartheid, or the separation of those who express or hold religiously based views from those who espouse views that are deemed politically correct.[10]

Tolerance and Diversity, Except For . . .

Political correctness results in the restriction of expression. The tolerance and respect for diversity espoused by PC are, in fact, reserved only for views and expression that are politically correct. Political correctness is only tolerant of like-minded viewpoints, and the mandated respect for diversity allows no room for the expression of politically incorrect ideas. By definition, PC must stifle the expression of all viewpoints that deviate from accepted views.

For example, a survey of PC-inspired speech codes in place at 384 publicly funded colleges and universities reveals that 108 of the institutions forbid "advocacy of offensive or outrageous viewpoints."[11] Although these speech restrictions will likely be invalidated if challenged in the courts, "offensive" views regarding the sanctity of human life and the sin of homosexual conduct could be silenced under these codes.

The effects of political correctness thus extend well beyond eliminating discrimination and insult. Political correctness ultimately will silence all views deemed to be "incorrect." A recent controversy in the music industry provides a clear example of this point:

[Steve] Vaus's song "We Must Take America Back," a response to deteriorating conditions in his adopted hometown of San Diego, was pulled from the airwaves in late July 1992 by RCA, which had signed a contract with Vaus for the rights to this ten-song album less than one month before. RCA was initially enthusiastic about the tune, which had risen to the top of call-in request charts in cities around the United States following its release last spring. But objections from programmers at major radio stations to the "controversial philosophical content" of the song [a call for citizen action] led RCA to dump Vaus's album, cancel his contract, and prevent him from re-releasing or even recording his material for five years. . . .

[According to Vaus,] "Since when does a record company allow anyone to dictate the content of its releases? . . . Ice-T's singing about killing cops, and Sister Souljah's rapping for genocide, and I can't sing about God and country?"

As this episode makes clear, Congress and criminals are not to be criticized, but the violence and obscenity advocated by "artists" like Ice-T and Sister Souljah, as well as 2 Live Crew, Public Enemy, Madonna, and most recently 2Pac, are protected under the First Amendment. From 2 Live Crew's graphically and misogynously sexual 1990 album *As Nasty As They Wanna Be* to Public Enemy's 1991 video for the rap "By the Time I Get to Arizona," which depicted the shooting and poisoning of public officials who declined to approve a public holiday honoring Martin Luther King, Jr.; from Madonna's fall 1992 release of the aptly named "Erotica" to Ice-T's infamous "Cop Killer," which Time Warner, the parent company of his record label *Sire*, pulled from his album *Body Count* only after Ice-T himself gave into popular pressure—these examples of "creative expression" make any protest about the "controversial philosophical content" of Vaus's lyrics seem absurd. Indeed, in comparison to the words of "Souljas's Story" by rapper Tupac Amaru Shakur, known as 2Pac, Vaus's ditty is mere child's play. "Cops on my tail so I bail till I dodge 'em / They finally pull me over and I laugh / Remember Rodney King and I blast on his punk a— / Now I got a murder case." *These* lines, which incited one Ronald Howard to fatally shoot a state trooper who had pulled him over for a routine traffic stop near Victoria, Texas, last year, are controversial.[12]

With the marketplace of ideas effectively censored of all but the "correct" ones, the very formation of beliefs will, in the end, be impaired.

This booklet will explore the origins and concerns of the PC phenomenon, its status with respect to legal challenges, the effects of PC on religious persons, and, finally, will provide ideas for how religious persons can challenge the negative aspects of PC in order to preserve their right to express their religious views freely, even where such views are not politically correct.

Origins and Concerns

"Neutral" Terminology

Political correctness began as a way to make academic institutions more open, diverse, and egalitarian. The PC movement was envisioned as an attempt to include all of the elements of America's culture through manipulations of a common language and education. The use of terms such as "native American" instead of "Indian," or "African-American" instead of "black," was offered to help combat prejudice by using people's chosen terms for identifying groups to which they belonged.[13] As one author summed up the premise: "Common courtesy dictates one should address people by the names they prefer."[14]

Perhaps more importantly, studies showed gender-neutral language or references to prominent figures in casebooks and children's storybooks could make a difference in perceptions.[15]

Expanding the curriculum at universities and contents of magazines to include "multiculturalism" was intended to add to the enrichment of students and readers, especially those curriculums previously limited to studies strictly based upon European history. Educating people about the many aspects of the civilization of man could only be beneficial, it was argued, in an increasingly diverse society and interconnected world.[16]

The goal of fostering respect for this diversity also spurred the adoption of so-called hate speech codes at universities across the United States.[17] Such codes were often also justified as a response to concerns about the rising numbers of violent acts and harassment occurring on college campuses.[18]

Hate speech codes[19] were often premised on the belief that racist speech, for example, "creates an intimidating, hostile, or demeaning environment" that "interfere[s] with an individual's academic efforts [and] participation in University sponsored extra-curricular activities."[20] Some proponents argued that racist speech caused discrete and serious harm to racial minorities and other victim groups.[21] Finally, it appears that the adoption of racial harassment policies can be a university's effort to symbolize its commitment to tolerance and nondiscrimination.[22]

Although some of the original intentions of the PC movement may have been worthy, the negative effects and implications of the movement are nonetheless far-reaching. Some of these are discussed below.

Campus Freedom of Expression Is Limited

The first casualty of the PC movement has been freedom of expression at America's college and university campuses. Traditionally, college and university campuses were precisely where nontraditional thoughts and philosophies were given birth as well as wide berth. In many cases, controversial student movements resulted in positive social change. However, the mandates of PC choke off free expression and thus the development of ideas and responses to society's problems. The following incidents demonstrate what is happening on America's college and university campuses.

• A homosexual student group hung thirty to forty anti-Catholic posters around the Carnegie Mellon University campus in Pennsylvania.[23] The poster's banner headline read "STOP THE CHURCH" and featured two photographs of New York Cardinal John J. O'Connor. One of the photographs labeled the cardinal as a "Public Health Menace," while the other showed the cardinal with a condom, and urged the reader to "Know Your Scumbags."[24] Although the poster did not identify the campus group responsible for its display, printed across the bottom of the poster was the message: "We're here, We're queer, We're funded by your Student Activities Fee."[25]

Three Carnegie Mellon students, including Patrick Mooney, paused to read one of the posters and began to discuss their disbelief that any campus group would display this poster.[26] Tim Saternow, a visiting assistant professor of drama, interjected himself into the students' conversation by asserting, "There's a bit of truth to it."[27] According to Mr. Saternow, Mr. Mooney then responded by loudly asking, "Why are you homosexuals attacking the Church?"[28] As he later wrote in a complaint to university officials, Mr. Saternow felt harassed by Mr. Mooney's "loud denouncements of homosexuals attacking the church" and Mr. Mooney's assertions as to "what real truth was."[29] The encounter is claimed to have lasted less than sixty seconds.[30]

Although facilitating the exchange of opinions on a topic of public interest might appear to be the business of a university, on the campus of Carnegie Mellon University, as well as at colleges with similar speech codes, "some opinions are more equal than others."[31] When Mr. Saternow injected himself into a student conversation by claiming that the most prominent leader of the Catholic Church in the United States was a "scumbag," it was protected as free speech. However, when Mr. Mooney responded by disagreeing with Mr. Saternow in defense of his religious faith, the disagreement led the university to charge Mooney with "harassment on the basis of sexual orientation" under the university's speech code.[32]

Mr. Saternow's complaint did not accuse the students of using any derogatory words for homosexuals.[33] Instead, Mr. Saternow's greatest offense came from Mr. Mooney's alleged use of the phrase "you homosexuals" in his question "Why are you homosexuals attacking the Church?"[34] Mr. Saternow apparently alleges that the students included him as part of the homosexual rights movement in the context of his defense of a poster hung by gay rights activists. Although Mr. Saternow displayed a pink triangle on his book bag, a political symbol of gay activism, Mr. Saternow charged that it was harassment for him to be recognized as a homosexual.[35]

Mr. Mooney was eventually exonerated on the charge of verbal harassment. However, it took the university disciplinary committee three and one-half hours in a closed-door session to conclude that Mr. Mooney had the right to speak out against the poster and to defend his faith.[36]

• In a well-publicized case at the University of Michigan, a graduate student was charged with violating the school's Policy on Discrimination and Discriminatory Harassment of Students in the University Environment for stating during class his belief that homosexuality was a "disease," and that he intended "to develop a counseling plan for changing gay clients to straight."[37]

Many other examples of incidents such as these may be found at universities and colleges throughout the United States.

Training of Future Leaders

The suppression of free expression on college and university campuses will likely deprive the society at large of positive social change and innovation because the intellectual and philosophical underpinnings necessary for such change and innovation will not be permitted to develop.

Another aspect of such deprivation is that America's future leaders will not be educated as to the religious and philosophical heritage inherent in this country's foundation and development as a great nation. There is legitimate concern that as a result of the influence of political correctness, many of the important values and precepts of our forebears will not be included in the education of the nation's future leaders. America's future leaders will be ignorant of, or at least will not respect, many of America's cherished religious and philosophical underpinnings. Thus, they will be unable to preserve them or to use them as they decide how to lead the country.

Censorship in America's Culture

Although the movement originated on America's college and university campuses, PC is spreading through the mass media and into the workplaces, churches, public schools, and social gatherings of America. Its result has been discrimination and censorship of both speech and behavior in America's general culture.

One of the worthy goals of the political correctness movement is to eliminate prejudice. However, under the PC agenda, it is not, as *Newsweek* magazine reports, "enough for a student to refrain from insulting homosexuals or other minorities. He or she would be expected to 'affirm' their presence on campus and to study their literature and culture alongside that of Plato, Shakespeare and Locke. This agenda is broadly shared by most organizations of minority students, feminists and gays."[38]

This is the crux of the problem. The elimination of prejudice is a worthy goal. But the motivation for eliminating prejudice, so far as speech is concerned, must be *internal*. When the *state* changes language and suppresses speech to accommodate its political agenda, freedom is imperiled.

Prior to the Carnegie Mellon poster incident mentioned above, Patrick Mooney was terminated from his position as a residence hall assistant when he was a sophomore because he refused to affirm a belief that was in conflict with his religious faith.[39] As a part of his job, Mr. Mooney was required to attend a "Gay, Lesbian and Bisexual Issues" sensitivity training session. However, it was not sufficient that Mr. Mooney simply attend the session; it was also necessary that he affirm the coequal status of homosexual and heterosexual relationships by wearing a pin with a symbol of the homosexuality movement.[40]

Mr. Mooney was faced with a choice. He could wear a pin symbolizing a belief at odds with his religious faith, or lose his job. Mr. Mooney left the "sensitivity training" session refusing to wear the button and was fired.[41]

The standard consequence of a PC code violation is "sensitivity training" and not a more traditional "punishment" for inappropriate conduct. Rather than punish, these sessions aim to "correct" the thoughts and ideas of the offender.[42] The goal is not to minimize the future speech code infractions, but to change the viewpoint of the offender.

In the 1979 afterword to his book *Fahrenheit 451*, Ray Bradbury wrote:

The point is obvious. There is more than one way to burn a book. And the world is full of people running about with lit matches. Every minority, be it Baptist/Unitarian, Irish/Italian/Octogenarian/Zen Buddhist, Zionist/Seventh-Day Adventist, Women's Lib/Republican, Mattachine/Four Square Gospel feels it has the will, the right, the duty to douse the kerosene, light the fuse. . . . Fire-Captain Beatty, in my novel *Fahrenheit 451*, described how the books were burned first by minorities, each ripping a page or a paragraph from this book, then that, until the day when the books were empty and the minds shut and the libraries closed forever.[43]

The temperature at which paper burns is 451 degrees Fahrenheit. It was Ray Bradbury's prediction that future societies would burn books in order to conceal the truth. However, with political correctness, contemporary society is attempting to suppress *ideas* even before they can be spoken or written.

Therefore, in the end, the crucial question concerns those who are politically "incorrect"—those who intentionally or unintentionally fail to conform to the "community spirit."

Although many people have some idea as to what comments would be derogatory or insulting to certain groups of individuals, "acceptable" language changes with the times. The difficulties in ascertaining "preferred" terminology can be seen in the entry for the term "Afro-American," in the

Dictionary of Cautionary Words and Phrases' which contained the cautionary note, "Preferred by some, but not universally accepted."[44] Thus, someone who used the term "Afro-American" could be shunned for using a term not universally accepted by the people it describes.

Determining what terms are and are not acceptable is not the only problem. A similar issue involves the question of where the line would be drawn. There are obvious discrepancies in what can and what cannot be said under PC requirements.

For example, racist comments are not allowed by white individuals but may be permitted by black individuals. Thus, the Whitney Museum's "New York Biennial" exhibit in 1993 featured this advice in cut-out letters two feet high: "In the rich man's house the only place to spit is in his face," and tags that visitors received in exchange for their admittance fee (which ostensibly had to be worn as evidence that one's admission fee had been paid) contained fragments of the sentence "I can't imagine ever wanting to be white."[45] There is little doubt that substitution of the word "black" for "white" would have generated a response adverse enough to have shut down the exhibition.

Under PC, may a man who holds pro-life views make negative comments about a woman who holds pro-abortion views? One could argue his comments are aimed at the woman's view on abortion, while another could argue his comments are sexist based.

What about a Black Muslim who disparages a black Baptist?

Another example includes the use of the word *community*. Once again, the *Dictionary of Cautionary Words and Phrases* contains a warning concerning the use of this word. "[The term *community*] implies a monolithic culture in which people, act, think, and vote in the same way. Do not use, as in Asian, Hispanic, black, or gay community. Be more specific as to what the group is: e.g., black residents in a northside neighborhood."[46]

Further, some words thought to be demeaning may actually be favored by some. For example, an article in the *New York Times* reported some gay rights activists preferred the term *queer* in that it was thought to be defiant and empowering.[47]

Examples taken to the extreme include the "politically correct" wording "hair disadvantaged," or "follicularly challenged," which means bald, or the term "vertically challenged," which means short.[48] A deputy prosecutor in Hawaii was sanctioned for "sexist" remarks during a trial because he assumed a coworker of a member of the jury pool was a "mailman."[49]

Examples of speech that would or would not be prohibited were given by one advocate of hate speech regulations. They include: "anti-white speech by blacks would be permitted, but not anti-Semitic speech by blacks or whites. Zionism would be permitted only to the extent that it 'aris[es] out of the Jewish experience of persecution,' but not where it is a statement of white supremacy."[50]

This is not to downplay the importance of respecting the wishes of minority or other groups in their preference of descriptive words, but the examples above demonstrate some of the extremes of political correctness and its potential for abuse.

Society should be an even playing ground for all to use to make and change laws. As long as there is a balanced perspective and true tolerance for the expression of all views, diversity and freedom survive.

However, once any group takes the helm of political power to the exclusion of others—whether that group be carrying a swastika, a hammer and sickle, a peace symbol, the Bible, or a pink triangle—then, as we have seen in the past, the nonconformists become outcasts and outlaws.

Extremist Steam Valves and Underground Thoughts

Regulating speech also creates resentment, and censorship measures often have the effect of glorifying extremist speakers.[51] Attempts at suppression too often result in attention and publicity that would have otherwise not been garnered.

Some studies have shown that governmental attempts to censor speech, for whatever reasons, often make the speech more appealing.[52] As one scholar notes, "Advocates of hate speech regulations do not seem to realize that their own attempts to suppress speech increase public interest in the ideas they are trying to stamp out."[53]

This is reflected in the popularity of radio and television speakers such as Rush Limbaugh, Howard Stern, and others. Their popularity is undoubtedly at least partially the result of their acting as steam valves to speak for those who no longer dare to speak for themselves.[54]

Pressure from the PC movement also forces thoughts underground that are viewed as politically "incorrect" and removes a barometer of the attitudes of society. Some argue that "racist speech can be used as a 'social thermometer' that allows us to 'register the presence of disease within the body politic.'"[55] Ideas that are seen as wrong and unjust, therefore, are much more difficult to respond to when they are not openly admitted.[56] Knowledge about the extent of racism may be of use in determining what some call the best "healing" measures, whether they be in the form of education, antidiscrimination laws, or more economic opportunities.[57] Past experience has shown that the public airing of racist comments has resulted in community efforts to redress the bigotry that underlies the expression.[58] The alternative is to pretend the sentiments do not exist, thus permitting them to fester and grow. Sooner or later the underground tension erupts.

As noted by an author discussing hate speech laws and codes, "by targeting the most superficial expressions of such deep-seated attitudes, the codes apply a Band-Aid to a problem requiring major surgery."[59] Generally, the democratic process works best when critical discourse is allowed. Group discussion allows the airing of concerns, which in turn makes it possible to address them.

Further, permitting racist or other negative or harmful speech actually helps strengthen tolerance and restraint. A society hesitant to jump the gun against provocations such as racist speech will be less quick to bypass moral standards in time of stress or danger. An example of this could be seen during the 1950s, where people were quick to label fellow workers and friends as "Communists" in order to avoid being blacklisted. "Only a tolerant society can be counted on to refrain from the frenzied search for scapegoats so characteristic of human experience."[60] Both those imposing political correctness and those silenced will have to relearn the lesson of tolerating diverse or conflicting views in order to prevent another "McCarthy era."

Stifling Truth

Perhaps the most serious threat to the culture posed by the PC movement is that it stifles the discovery of truth. Free speech is often the best way to uncover truth.[61] By allowing a free marketplace of ideas, open to even the most offensive ideas and expressions, truth will generally ultimately triumph.[62]

Speech codes and the PC movement destroy the free flow of ideas. Individuals become afraid to speak up for fear of being ostracized or perhaps even being punished under some speech code.

For example, many students fear going before a college tribunal because of possible career-jeopardizing punishment.[63] In one notable incident, it has been reported that a male Brown University sophomore was suspended from the university for four and one-half years for leaving three vulgar messages on a female student's answering machine after a dispute.[64]

A Wesleyan University student has written:

> These incidents and many others make it clear that student judicial boards have become increasingly politicized to punish those who dare to stray from the prevailing ideological hegemony.

25

. . . The vagueness of the offenses and the possibility of ominous, complicated proceedings before the mock courts have created the desired air of uncertainty and intimidation, in writings by students, in oral presentations in class, in physical relationships, and in private dealing with other students who might report to the speech police.[65]

The culture of forbidden speech is continuing.[66] The editor of a student paper at the University of Wisconsin at Milwaukee found students were less willing to discuss frankly the school's code once it went into effect.[67] In another event, columnist Nat Hentoff recounts that a Brown University graduate student felt compelled to tell incoming students that "there are some things that are simply not discussed here."[68] In some cases, students are even pressured into majoring in areas that are in accordance with their race and gender and other elements of their "background."[69]

Regardless of actual speech code requirements, the mere threat of being rebuked can have a serious, chilling effect on classroom discussions. At George Mason University law school, students themselves launched a petition drive seeking to ban a particular word from all classrooms under all circumstances after a law professor illustrated a "discussion of hurtful speech that might merit litigation."[70] As one author has observed: "Law school professors report an enormous unwillingness among students to even argue hypothetically for the 'wrong' side in matters that touch upon [political correctness] because of a fear of being labeled an -*ist* of some sort: racist, sexist, heterosexist, classist, ableist."[71]

The pressure to conform to PC requirements, and thus limit the free flow of discussion in the classroom, is not limited to students. At Harvard University, for example, two professors stopped teaching a course on race relations after being accused of insensitivity, among other things, to African-Americans because one professor read from a plantation owner's diary without giving equal time to the recollections of a slave.[72]

As a result of PC requirements, truth and, ultimately, freedom suffer. Indeed, commentators have noted that the new rules at universities are "fostering a decline in tolerance and a rise in intellectual intimidation."[73] Benno Schmidt, Jr., president of Yale University, has summarized the concern:

> When offensiveness is ground for suppression, a lethal and utterly openended engine of censorship is loosed. Its impact will be felt not only by those whose speech is punished; the greater problem is the vastly greater number of speakers who will steer clear of possible punishment by steering clear of controversial or unpopular views. The chilling effects of vague powers to punish offensive speech are likely to be far more damaging to freedom of expres-

sion than the actual application of such rules.[74]

In light of history's record of human fallibility in recognizing truth, freedom of expression must include freedom for all expression and not just the promulgation of one view as the only and correct one.

The Constitution, the Courts, and Free Speech

Speech Protected by the First Amendment

At their most basic level, the speech provisions of the First Amendment encompass the right to advocate ideas, to speak freely, to associate with whomever one chooses, and to petition the government for redress of grievances.[75] Such activities are protected against blanket prohibitions and restrictions based upon government opposition to the content of the ideas being expressed.[76]

The purposes of the First Amendment are fulfilled when an individual or institution does not suppress constitutionally protected speech, but instead counters by exercising First Amendment rights.

Particularly suspect are "prior restraints" that prohibit expression before it occurs.[77] Such restrictions are always subject to a "heavy presumption against [their] constitutional validity."[78] The very concept of PC is a prior restraint on speech and must be recognized as such. Whether formal or informal, PC restrictions prohibit certain speech before it occurs.

The right to free speech protects the rights of the speaker. But equally important, the right also protects the general public interest in having information from a free marketplace of ideas.[79]

The Supreme Court has stressed the importance of this latter interest: "That falsehoods may be exposed through the process of education and discussion is essential to free government. Those who won our independence had confidence in the power of free and fearless reasoning and communication of ideas to discover and spread political and economic truth."[80] Free speech has, then, as one of its functions to protect society from the errors in judgment that occur when only one side of an issue is considered.[81]

The PC movement has led to a line of cases dealing with statutes and ordinances that place restrictions on so-called hate speech. Such speech is generally defined as any form of expression that insults or provokes violence on the basis of race, color, creed, religion, or gender.

Advocates of such restrictions often argue that the so-called fighting words doctrine justifies limits on hate speech. The fighting words doctrine permits limitations on language which one knows or has reason to know arouses anger, alarm, or resentment in others. The Supreme Court has recently decided two significant cases dealing with this issue.

In *R.A.V. v. St. Paul*, the Court *struck down* an ordinance that prohibited forms of expression "one knows or has reason to know arouses anger, alarm or resentment in others on the basis of race, color, creed, religion or gender."[82]

Fighting words may not be prohibited because they communicate a particular idea. Rather, fighting words may constitutionally be prohibited because they represent an unacceptable mode of expression *regardless of the view expressed.*[83]

In *Wisconsin v. Mitchell*, the Supreme Court *upheld* a state statute that imposed increased sentences for persons convicted of crimes in which the victim was intentionally selected because of race.[84]

The Court said that the Wisconsin statute is valid because it punishes specific types of *actions* based on the form they take, whereas the St. Paul ordinance is unconstitutional because it *restricts the expression of certain ideas* because of the content they contain.

As a critical element of a free society (the very formation of belief), free speech in a university setting is especially protected.[85] Justice William Brennan has written:

Our Nation is deeply committed to safeguarding academic freedom, which is of transcendent value to all of us and not merely to the teachers concerned. That freedom is therefore a special concern of the First Amendment, which does not tolerate laws that cast a pall of orthodoxy over the classroom. . . . The classroom is peculiarly the "marketplace of ideas." The Nation's future depends upon leaders trained through wide exposure to that robust exchange of ideas which discovers truth "out of a multitude of tongues, [rather] than through any kind of authoritative selection."[86]

Thus, the United States Supreme Court has repeatedly prohibited public schools from suppressing the expression of certain types of views, even when those views are offensive.[87]

An indivisible concept of free speech is the premise that words that are merely offensive may not be prohibited.[88] For example, in the flag-burning case that received a good deal of national attention,[89] and which continues to generate strong feelings, the Supreme Court struck down the Texas flag desecration law, stating:

If there is a bedrock principle underlying the First Amendment, it is that the government may not prohibit the expression of an idea simply because society finds the idea itself offensive or disagreeable.[90]

After all, said the Court, "one man's vulgarity is another's lyric."[91]

In another controversial and emotionally charged case,[92] despite the city's restrictions otherwise, a Nazi march was permitted through a predominantly Jewish neighborhood where many Holocaust survivors lived. Although the march would have been offensive to most people, the Constitution and its free speech requirements made it necessary for the parade to be permitted.

Unfortunately, this understanding of the Constitution's protections and requirements continues to be under attack. Although the matter of abortion has the highest profile of these cases, many other PC views are in direct conflict with sincerely held religious beliefs (such as homosexuality or abstinence, for example).

The recent Florida abortion protest case is a clear signal of what may be the resolution of conflicts between PC views and such religious beliefs.

In October 1991, the Women's Health Center (Center) petitioned Florida's Eighteenth Judicial Circuit Court to restrict the abortion protest speech of Operation Rescue and others (Operation Rescue), outside a Melbourne, Florida, abortion facility.[93] A careful study of the facts determined by the Florida Circuit Court reveals that it was not access to abortion, *but the rights of an unwilling listener in a traditional public forum that created the issue before that court.*

The facts of the case as stipulated by the parties and findings of the Florida Circuit Court indicate that the protests of Operation Rescue and other pro-life activists were generally restricted to the public sidewalk, public right-of-way, and a public road at the clinic's northern property line.[94] The Florida Circuit Court did not find that access to the clinic had been blocked by Operation Rescue, but instead described only an occasional momentary delay for cars entering the clinic parking lot, necessary to allow Operation Rescue pickets to move out of the way of oncoming vehicles as cars would enter the lot by crossing over the right-of-way running parallel to clinic grounds.[95]

The Florida Circuit Court's findings reveal that the momentary delay in driving into the parking lot was nothing more than the momentary delay necessary to allow the pickets to remove themselves from the right-of-way.[96] There was no physical blockade of the Melbourne abortion facility by pro-life demonstrators.[97] In this way, the Florida Circuit Court indicated that entrance to the clinic building was not blocked by the protests of Operation Rescue, and entrance to the clinic parking lot was subject only to a delay having the frequency of "sometimes" and a "momentary" duration.

However, when justifying the expanding scope of the Amended Permanent Injunction, this occasional, momentary delay was characterized by the Florida Circuit Court as "imped-[ing] and obstruct[ing] both staff and patients from entering the clinic."[98] This conclusion of the circuit court seems to be a mischaracterization of the underlying facts found by that same judicial body, and it is the underlying found facts and not the conclusions drawn by the Florida Circuit Court that reveal the true nature of this dispute.

The protests of Operation Rescue at the Melbourne facility did not deny patients their legal right to obtain abortions: there was no physical blockade of the clinic by Operation Rescue, and access to the abortion facility continued to be available throughout the protests.[99] In the absence of any denial of clinic access by Operation Rescue, the patients' rights were most accurately characterized as those of the unwilling listener, much the same issue that the courts have faced in the flag burning and Nazi march cases already discussed. The task of the court was to balance the rights of the speaker and unwilling listener in a traditional public forum.

Beyond the Florida Circuit Court's misplaced attempt to combat occasional "momentary hesitation" as people drove into the clinic parking lot, the court justified the injunction as necessary for the protection of patient health and safety from noise emanating from protests outside the clinic.[100] Demonstrations at the facility drew both anti-abortion and pro-clinic supporters, often resulting in heated exchanges between individuals from both groups.[101] During the demonstrations, Operation Rescue "and those aligned with them, remained primarily in the public right-of-way (paved and unpaved). The pro-choice people would be on the edge of the clinic's lawn and parking lot (private property) but occasionally attempt[ed] to share the sidewalk with the opposition."[102] The Florida Circuit Court found that the noise of the demonstrations interfered with the operation of the clinic and the well-being of patients, concluding that the noise "should be limited and restrained."[103]

Importantly, the Florida court, however, did not find the threat of noise sufficiently compelling to include both pro-life and pro-choice demonstrators within the restrictions of the injunction, although both groups created the "noise" admonished by the court.[104]

The amended permanent injunction was purposely drawn to encompass only pro-life speech by explicitly enjoining Operation Rescue and other pro-life organizations, specific pro-life activist individuals, and "all persons acting in concert or participation with them or on their behalf. . . ."[105] In formulating the injunction, it was the intent of the court to address only the speech of pro-life, and not pro-abortion, demonstrators and to restrict the expression of pro-life viewpoints to the other side of the street.[106] No restrictions were placed on pro-abortion demonstrators.

In reviewing the Florida injunction, the Eleventh Circuit Court of Appeals stated:

> Such a restriction is no more viewpoint-neutral than one restricting the speech of the Republican Party, the state Republican Party, George Bush, Bob Dole, Jack Kemp and all persons acting in concert or participation with them or on their behalf. The practical effect of this section of the injunction was to assure that while "pro-life" speakers would be arrested, "pro-choice" demonstrators would not. This is apparently precisely what occurred.[107]

In striking the injunction, the Eleventh Circuit Court defended the expression of offensive ideas:

> It is tempting, of course, to entertain the argument that the speech in this case is disruptive, discourteous, and offensive, but that is irrelevant. The Supreme Court recently reminded us, . . . "'The fact that society may find speech offensive is not a sufficient reason for suppressing it. Indeed, if it is the speaker's opinion that gives offense, that consequence is a reason for according it constitutional protection.'" *Hustler Magazine, Inc. v. Falwell*, 485 U.S. 46, 55 (1988) *quoting FCC v. Pacifica Foundation*, 438 U.S. 726, 745

(1978). "'If there is a bedrock principle underlying the First Amendment, it is that the Government may not prohibit the expression of an idea simply because society finds the idea itself offensive or disagreeable.'" *United States v. Eichman,* 496 U.S. _____ , 110 S. Ct. 2404, 2410 (1990) *quoting Texas v. Johnson,* 491 U.S. 397 (1989). We protect much that offends in the name of free speech—we cannot refuse such protection to those who find abortion morally reprehensible.[108]

However, on subsequent review, the U.S. Supreme Court did not agree. Although the Court has protected expression through nude dancing and flag burning and upheld the rights of Nazis to march through the neighborhoods of concentration camp survivors, the Court ruled that the pro-life demonstrations could be regulated to eliminate even the momentary hesitation at the ingress of the parking lot of an abortion clinic.[109] The Court's decision was undeniably based upon the content of the expression that conflicted with views that are currently politically correct.

PC versus Religious Expression— Religious Apartheid

The Media and "Fundamentalists"

The bombing of the World Trade Center and the deaths of Branch Davidians and federal agents in Waco, Texas, provided ample fodder for the media to equate "cultists" with "fundamental-ists" and lump them together as lunatics who should be locked up or otherwise restrained. Being a religious funda-mentalist of any type now means being politically incorrect, and the actions of the print and broadcast media will en-sure that the linkage is not undone.

The killings of Pensacola, Florida, abortion doctors in March 1993 and July 1994 provided further opportuni-ties to characterize all pro-life protes-ters as dangerous, self-righteous zealots. For example, Anthony Lewis, a *New York Times* columnist, wrote that "most antiabortion activists" are "reli-gious fanatics" who think "the end jus-tifies any means."[110]

In the aftermath of the deaths in Pensacola, John Leo of *U.S. News & World Report* writes:

> The words "terrorists," "cultists" and "fanatics" rained down on all sides. These are words that the abortion-rights lobby pushes journalists to use, and they do. . . . Syndicated columnist Ellen Goodman . . . wrote that radical antiabortion groups like Operation Rescue and Rescue America have to be dealt with as domestic terrorists as deadly as the ones who blew up the World Trade Center and as fanatic as the cultists in Waco.[111]

Religious Apartheid

As rejection of religion, and Chris-tianity in particular, continues to grow, few can deny that the media has played an important role in the stigmatization of religion as evil. Given that the majority of those who control the mainstream media in the United States appear to be zealously secular, it is no surprise that religion is being derided and removed from American public life.[112] One commentator has suggested that secular liberals have, in part, contributed to religious radicalism itself: "Some religious people sense that they are 'being shut off from civic participation'"[113]

Under the regime of political correctness, Christians largely remain the only group that may be publicly defamed with impunity. One apparent example involves labels used by the media (and even the government) to describe Christians. One such label is *sectarian*, a term that is hardly flattering, since one of its dictionary meanings is "a narrow or bigoted person." As Cornell professor Richard A. Baer, Jr., comments:

> [I]t is disturbing to note that the mass media regularly use the term to describe and label individual Americans and groups of Americans. Even more disturbing, however, is its use by the U.S. Supreme Court. Since roughly the end of World War II the highest tribunal of our land has used the term in a wide variety of cases as a synonym for the word *religious*.[114]

"[The term *sectarian*] is caste language," Baer continues, "a phrase that has been used throughout American history to keep the religious 'untouchables' in their proper place."[115]

> Just as ruling elites have used racial and sexual epithets to put down blacks and women, so they have used *sectarian* to exclude and marginalize those individuals and groups whose religious beliefs and practices did not correspond to their own vision of what was appropriate in the cultural marketplace.[116]

Labeling—and therefore dooming something as politically incorrect—is especially risky in a society that is so dominated by the electronic media. The way the media shapes public opinion (even to the point of electing presidents) brings into question the entire concept of free speech. As Dr. Judith Reisman writes:

> Speech is "permitted" by a wealthy oligarchy that controls and directs a media monopoly through various techniques, one of which is censorship. Ours is an image-addicted environment in which the consumer public tends to respond to classical Pavlovian conditioning, that is, continuous repetition of stimuli coupled with promises of emotional rewards or punishment. Through a successful public relations effort conducted by this corporate oligarchy, censored and controlled communications have been used to paralyze freedom of speech and of the press, causing these to become mere illusions, a part of a mythology the oligarchy strives to perpetuate.[117]

"So We Can Speak Louder"

Throughout the history of America, free speech has been the springboard to freedom and social change.

The free expression of ideas was important, for example, to the women's suffrage movement. During the 1960s, the civil rights movement depended on free speech principles. Martin Luther King and other civil rights champions spoke loudly and often, gathering others to support their cause. It was free expression that allowed important messages to be carried to the nation, even to those who found those messages to be highly offensive and threatening to their values and way of life. Members of the civil rights movement were in danger of losing their jobs and, in some cases, their lives as they were equated with Communists, subversives, and criminals by government officials. Indeed, "[o]nly strong principles of free speech and association could—and did—protect the drive for desegregation."[118]

Any restraint on speech holds the opportunity to endanger those who most need the ability to express their views. Thus, Aryeh Neier, a survivor of the Holocaust, decided to defend the American Civil Liberties Union's decision to fight for the rights of Nazis who wanted to march in a Jewish neighborhood; otherwise his speech could be endangered as well. Neier says:

If the Nazis are free to speak, they may win converts. It is possible that they will win so many adherents that they will attain the power to abolish freedom and destroy me. . . . The restraints that matter most to me are those which ensure that I cannot be squashed by power, unnoticed by the rest of the world. If I am in danger, I want to cry out to my fellow Jews and to all those I may be able to enlist as my allies. I want to appeal to the world's sense of justice. I want restraints which prohibit those in power from interfering with my right to speak, my right to publish, or my right to gather with others who also feel threatened. Those in power must not be allowed to prevent us from assembling and joining our voices together so we can speak louder and make sure that we are heard.[119]

A more fitting example of the need to protect free speech cannot be found. Protection of the right to cry out for justice is too great and too necessary to limit the expression of even those who are most despised. And, under PC, it is religious persons who are among those despised.

What You Can Do

Although PC as a *concept* is under growing legal and so-called intellectual criticism, the *practice of* PC is continuing and becoming more strictly enforced, both formally and informally. America's workplaces are enacting speech codes through personnel policies and sensitivity training classes. America's classrooms are censoring ideas by manipulating language and the terms used to teach our students. Even some churches and Christian organizations are diluting their messages by revising their vocabularies. Persons with politically incorrect views are no longer included in many social events.

As mentioned above, religious persons holding beliefs at odds with today's PC requirements are being excluded from America's dialogue. Religious apartheid has begun through the sanitization of language. Enforcement of PC beyond the dictates of language will not be forestalled by concessions. Following are several suggestions of what religious persons, particularly those with traditional Judeo- Christian values, may do to halt the spread of religious apartheid by resisting the tide of political correctness.

Understand the Problem

Religious persons are coming to a maturer understanding that the undergirding of American religious and political philosophy has changed. The prevailing philosophy of contemporary America is now secular. Religious persons are coming to understand that secularism is not compatible with Judeo-Christian beliefs and values.[120]

The dominance of secularism in contemporary America is resulting in the systematic legal attack on and prohibition of all religious expression in America's public places. Early court challenges to Christmas displays on public property and the "plastic reindeer" decisions that followed were merely the forerunners to the sanitization of America's public arena. Currently, no religious reference or historical religious symbol is too small to escape the current revisionism that is underway.

The PC regime is but another manifestation of this direction. Although PC proponents would deny that religious apartheid is PC's objective, it is undeniably its result. This is due to the nature of sincerely held religious belief. Either it is one's religious belief or it is not. If it is, then the belief is not subject to current social mores and PC requirements. The inevitable result is political incorrectness where religious beliefs collide with PC requirements.

Thus, religious persons must first understand the nature of the conflict and accept that political incorrectness is inevitable with respect to issues such as abortion, homosexuality, and sexuality, among others.

Understand PC
and Its Requirements

As noted throughout this booklet, the PC movement has some laudable goals. Religious persons must come to an understanding of these goals. Indeed, the avoidance of humiliation of and insult to others, accurate perceptions, and clearer interpersonal relationships should already be among the believer's goals. As also noted earlier, these goals should be internal and not even needful of government mandate.

But religious persons should also be wise and discerning. All of the PC goals are not laudable. Indeed, they are directed toward sanitizing the public arena, and, ultimately, the private arena of belief formation, of some very important religious principles. Believers must have an unimpaired understanding of these goals too.

Understand One's Own Religious Beliefs on Matters Encompassed by PC

Having attained an understanding of the problem and of the goals and concerns of PC, believers must attain a sure understanding of their own religious beliefs. Believers must examine their own views and separate any that are non-Christian from those religious beliefs that are sincerely held and based upon their best understandings of Judeo-Christian values. We must separate the problems that are political from the problems that are spiritual.

For example, one Christian activist blurted out to a group that his activism was the result of his desire to "drive all the queers out of the state." This is neither a Christian view nor a religious belief. It is a non-Christian attack on the sinner instead of the sin. We must ensure that our actions are based upon religious belief, not bigotry or prejudice.

Some pastors (and some in their congregations), emulating the Pharisees of the Bible, in effect withdraw from the world by subordinating their beliefs to PC dictates. Withdrawal is not Christianity. And, unfortunately, the withdrawal mentality apparent in many Christians who profess to be evangelical may well be linked to problems of belief. It is likely that many Christians are unsure if their beliefs will withstand the scrutiny of secular society and PC challengers.

Believers might be surprised at the results of such a self-examination. In any case, the exercise will be worthwhile. We can become better Christians, if nothing else. However, a clear and articulable understanding of one's religious beliefs will be vital in the struggle to defend the right to express them.

Express Political Incorrectness

Many of the problems of contemporary America stem from more than a century of church teaching that involvement in local church activities is more important than involvement in affairs and institutions of society. Many of the sermons, seminars, lectures, and books produced by the so-called Christian establishment today most often are con-

cerned with the spiritual enlightenment
and "self-help" of individual church-
goers. We must recapture the real di-
rective of Jesus Christ: Involvement in
all areas of the culture is a necessary
part of true Christianity. We must never
forget that there would be no United
States if the pastors of the 1700s had
not stood against the British and
preached revolution from the pulpit.[121]
Christians must each assume responsi-
bility for challenging PC requirements
where they conflict with sincerely held
religious beliefs.

Support Freedom of Expression for All

Many Christians hold as one-sided
a view of the First Amendment as do
PC adherents. They want to supress the
expression of ideas inimical to Christianity. This tendency to control the
speech of others is as wrong for Christians as it is for non-Christians. To ensure their own freedom of speech,
Christians must vigorously support the
right of others to express opposing
views. As noted earlier, this does not
mean that pornography or fighting
words should be defended. But it does
mean that Christians should be the
first to support a free marketplace of
ideas. After all, the Christian message
is truth and the free marketplace of
ideas is where truth will flourish.

The desire to control what is expressed sometimes results in censor-

ship on the part of Christians. This is a misguided effort. Christians should focus on putting books into libraries, not taking them out. Christians should focus on becoming involved in the arts, not destroying them. Such a shift toward the positive would more surely defeat PC censorship than would monastic retreat or Christian censorship.

Grab the Microphone

An important aspect of the marketplace of ideas involves the dissemination of ideas. Currently, the print and broadcast media are the carriers of PC. Many national newspapers have speech codes that are enforced internally and in their products. More importantly, the information they disseminate is PC itself. Thus, Christians must redouble their efforts to have their views accurately portrayed by the media.

An eighteen-month investigation conducted a few years ago documented abortion bias in the media.[122] According to the investigation, "the bias manifests itself, in print and on the air, almost daily in content, tone, choice of language or prominence of place."[123] Indeed: "Most major newspapers support abortion rights on their editorial pages, and reporters are decidedly pro-abortion. A 1985 *Los Angeles Times* poll found that 82 percent of journalists on newspapers of all sizes say they favor abortion rights. . . . The nations's largest newspaper chains, including the Gannett Foundation and the Knight Foundation, give money to pro-abortion groups."[124]

Another reporter believes that "[o]pposing abortion, in the eyes of most journalists . . . is not a legitimate, civilized position in our society."[125] Thus, "[j]ournalists tend to regard opponents of abortion as 'religious fanatics' and 'bug-eyed zealots.' . . . Among reporters, the anti-abortion movement is perceived as one of those . . . 'fringe' things somewhere out there in Middle America or Dixie. . . . Journalists . . . not only are not part of the anti-abortion movement, but don't know anyone who is."[126]

Christians must become journalists. They should regularly write serious and reasoned articles of publishable quality. They should prepare broadcast ads of high quality to air on local radio stations, and they should run well-done print ads in local newspapers and magazines. They should be in regular, favorable contact with local journalists.

Assert Your Rights

The United States has become a rights-minded society instead of a right-minded society. Christians have a duty to ensure that Judeo-Christian beliefs are not trampled in the PC stampede. Not only is this a duty owed to our culture, it is a duty owed to our children.

One way to accomplish this is to assert vigorously our own rights to freedom of expression and religion. Armed with a clear understanding of our beliefs and our rights, we must resist at every turn the legal, political, and cultural erosion of both.

This means expressing Judeo-Christian views through personal expression and through exercising the rights of a citizen. Christians should become involved in politics and statecraft.[127] Christians must become personally acquainted with their governmental representatives, the local school officials, community and church leaders, and everyone else with the power or ability to affect public policy and law.

Teach the Children

Most people are aware of the significant effect upon children of public school teaching, television, movies, books, and peers. Christians must be mindful that all of these influences are affected themselves by PC dictates and contemporary mores. Thus, parents must understand where such influences depart from those that they wish to affect their children. They must discuss these differences with their children and teach them to be wise and discerning.

Once children are past their very young years, Christian parents must cease shielding their children from ideas. *Ideas*, it must be stressed, are different from *graphic images*. Most children can handle ideas before they can handle graphic images about controversial subjects such as abortion, sex, and homosexuality. Parents must teach children how to analyze and evaluate ideas in the context of Judeo-Christian beliefs and principles. Parents must understand that their children are perhaps the most vulnerable of all to PC requirements and that it is the duty of parents to equip their children with the skills to preserve their rights to expression and religious belief.

Hold Your Church Accountable

The lack of resistance on the part of Christian churches during the 1930s to the Nazi state's Jewish policies has been the subject of extensive and still unconcluded literature. The Nazis understood early that the churches took their stand not on the issue of human rights of all Jews, but on an expedient and self-serving concern for "Christian Jews." The churches, by their submission to expediency and their lack of political involvement, were eventually neutralized by the state.

A small town near where I live recently passed a city ordinance that will require subordination of sincerely held religious beliefs opposing homosexuality to what amounts to a homosexual affirmative action plan for city contractors. In debating whether to comment on the proposed ordinance, the deacons of one of the largest churches in the community lamented that "if we take a stand on this issue, we will have to take a stand on all these issues." That comment should speak for itself, and Christians should not permit their churches to use such a rationale for inaction. Churches must not revise their theology to suit PC requirements.

Religious Correctness

To reflect their love for God, believers must love others as they love themselves. Such love requires "otherness," a focus away from oneself and a total respect for others, as a way of reflecting Jesus Christ. This is the kind of expression and action that draws people toward the truth. It concerns what we may call "humanness." Indeed, a primary task for this generation of believers is keeping humanness in the human race—that is, to upgrade and then maintain the individual person's high place in the universe. This is *true* political correctness, for it is *religious correctness*.

If Christians shrink from this challenge, religious apartheid will become a universal reality. In South Africa, in the heyday of apartheid, nonwhite races had no voice in the affairs of state. People with religious convictions in the United States are facing the same situation. In America, the Judeo-Christian tradition was the foundation of our government. We must keep religious liberty vital as an influence in all realms of our culture. PC is but one aspect of the attack on religious liberty. Thus, it is an aspect we must resist.

Notes

1. Sam Walker, "Rejected Ad Triggers Dispute," *Christian Science Monitor*, 5 July 1994, 13.

2. Andy Dabilis, "Lexington Students Allowed to Rule on Disputed Ad," *Boston Globe*, 27 March 1994, Northwest Weekly section. The district's decision to reject the advertisement was made by the yearbook faculty advisor and delegated to student editors of the newspaper by the superintendent of schools.

3. Ibid.

4. Walker, "Rejected Ad Triggers Dispute," 13.

5. Ibid.; Andy Dabilis, "Lexington Students Allowed to Rule on Disputed Ad."

6. Andy Dabilis, "In Lexington, Backlash Greets Suit Over Abstinence Ad Refusal," *Boston Globe*, 1 May 1994, Northwest Weekly section, 9.

7. See, for example, introductory remarks adopted from Ward Parks, "The Freedom to Express 'Incorrect' Ideas Is Still Under Attack at Many Universities," *Los Angeles Daily Journal*, 31 December 1992, 6.

8. According to Barbara Kessler, of the *Dallas Morning News:*

   Controversies surrounding whether to change the sports team mascots illustrate a classic tale of political correctness. . . . [The Minnesota] Gophers will not host home games for nonconference teams with American Indian names, such as the North Dakota Fighting Sioux hockey team or the Florida

State Seminoles baseball team. Minnesota also has outlawed Indian mascots and nicknames in public schools, which were forced to change or lose public funding. The *Oregonian* newspaper in Portland and the *Minneapolis Star-Tribune* have banned the use of Indian sports monikers in stories, turning the Redskins into "the Washington team" and the Braves into "the Atlanta team" and so forth.

Barbara Kessler, "Mascot Mayhem," *Dallas Morning News*, 26 April 1994, 1C.

9. Two instances demonstrate the intensity of this activism.

[A] Long Island middle school . . . scuttled a production of "Peter Pan" for fear that it would offend Native Americans. (The script calls for little English kids to dress as Indians and sing the song "Ugg-a-Wugg.")

Steve Berg, "The High Priest of PC," *Star Tribune*, 20 May 1994, A20.

The headmistress of an elementary school in London refused a charity's offer of reduced-price tickets for her pupils to see the ballet "Romeo and Juliet" at the world-renowned Covent Garden ballet and opera house. The objection to "Romeo and Juliet" was made on the grounds that the story is a "blatantly heterosexual love story." The headmistress stated that she would not involve her pupils —all under eleven years of age—in heterosexual culture until books, movies, and the theater reflect all forms of sexuality.

Raymond R. Coffey, "Ban 'Romeo'? Wherefore Art Thou Orwell?" *Chicago Sun-Times*, 23 January 1994, 5.

10. For a discussion of religious apartheid in general, and a discussion of political correctness in particular, see John W. Whitehead, *Religious Apartheid* (Chicago: Moody, 1994).

11. Bill Marvel, "A Culture War," *Dallas Morning News*, 24 April 1994, 1A (survey conducted by the Freedom Forum First Amendment Center at Vanderbilt University).

12. Christine Haynes, "Taking America Back," *Chronicles*, January 1993, 43–44.

13. Strossen, "Thoughts on the Controversy over Politically Correct Speech" (hereinafter, "Politically Correct Speech"), 46 *S.M.U. Law Review* 119, 129–31 (1992).

14. Ibid., 128, quoting Wills, "Peeling Off Political Labels," *Sacramento Bee*, 28 December 1990, B11.

15. An example of how language could play a definitive role in group equality may be found in the women's suffrage movement.

    During the 1872 presidential election, Susan B. Anthony and a group of other women sought to cast their ballots at the polls in Rochester, New York. However, upon arrival Anthony was arrested, indicted, prosecuted, convicted, and fined. In rejecting Anthony's claim of being protected by the Fourteenth Amendment, government officials stated that "the use of the masculine pronouns, 'he,' 'his' and 'him' in all the constitutions and laws, is proof that only men were meant to be included in their provisions." See Strossen, "Politically Correct Speech," 128–29, quoting Susan B. Anthony, "Women's Right to Vote," reprinted in *The American Reader: Words That Moved a Nation*, ed. Diane Ravitch (San Francisco: Harper Collins, 1991), 160–62.

16. Not all agree with this view. For example, an essay in *Time* magazine notes:

    > Talk of mosaics and quilts is both an attempt to describe the way America is headed and an effort to hurry it along. The description is inaccurate, and in a world of ungorgeous mosaics and fraying quilts, the goal is undesirable. The U.S. has had historic success with heavy bursts of immigration interspersed with decades of digestion, but only because people are asked to check their identity at the door. If the mild-mannered Czechs and Slovaks couldn't hold a multiethnic country together, and if the even milder-mannered Canadians are having trouble, we

> Americans should have second thoughts about becoming a true mosaic. Fortunately we're not one yet, except at the level of boiler plate. Let's hope we never take our speeches seriously.

Richard Brookhiser, "The Melting Pot Is Still Simmering," *Time*, 1 March 1993, 72.

17. For a listing of institutions, both public and private, that adopted hate speech codes or positions advocating the tenets of the PC movement, see Hyde and Fishman, "The Collegiate Speech Protection Act of 1991: A Response to New Intolerance in the Academy," 37 *Wayne Law Review* 1469, 1470–71 nn. 5–6 (1991).

18. For some examples of racial incidents on college campuses, see Lawrence, "If He Hollers Let Him Go: Regulating Racist Speech on Campus," 1990 *Duke Law Journal* 431, 431–34 (1990); Matsuda, "Public Response to Racist Speech: Considering the Victim's Story," 87 *Michigan Law Review* 2320, 2333 n. 71 (1989).

19. Although various courts have ruled hate speech codes and hate crimes laws unconstitutional, PC continues on both a formal and an informal basis. For example, even though the University of Michigan's hate speech code was declared unconstitutional, many university codes remain in place.

20. The quoted language was taken from the University of Michigan's Policy on Discrimination and Discriminatory Harassment in the University Environment, which is cited in *Doe v. University of Michigan*, 721 F. Supp. at 856.

21. Sedler, "The Unconstitutionality of Campus Bans on 'Racist Speech': The View from Without and Within," 53 *Univ. of Pittsburgh Law Review* 631 (1992); see, for example, Lawrence, 446–48, 462–66.

22. See Matsuda, 2322.

23. Carol Innerst, "Student Didn't Harass Gay, School Finds," *Washington Times*, 7 April 1994, A4.

24. "Campus Sensitivity Excludes Religious Interests," *Times-Picayune*, 30 March 1994, B7.

25. Innerst, "Student Didn't Harass Gay, School Finds," A4.

26. Joyce Price, "Student-Teacher Poster Tiff Draws Harassment Charge," *Washington Times*, 30 March 1994, A3.

27. "Campus Sensitivity," A4. (The student, however, recalls the professor's assertion as "It's the truth." Price, "Poster Tiff.")

28. Editorial, "Cowardly Lions in PC Land," *Washington Times*, 2 April 1994, D2. Mr. Mooney, however, denies directing his question at "you homosexuals."

29. Ibid.

30. "Campus Sensitivity Excludes Religious Interests," B7.

31. "Cowardly Lions in PC Land."

32. Ibid.

33. Ibid.

34. Ibid.

35. Ibid.

36. Price, "Poster Tiff."

37. See *Doe v. University of Michigan*, 721 F. Supp. at 852, 865 (E.D. Mich. 1989). The graduate student was not a party to the case.

38. Jerry Adler, "Taking Offense," *Newsweek*, 24 December, 1990, 48.

39. Carol Innerst, "Anti-PC Student 2, Carnegie-Mellon 0" *Washington Times*, 7 July 1994, A1.

40. Ibid. See also definition of heterosexism at n. 103, *infra*.

41. Ibid. Mr. Mooney sued the university and the suit was settled out of court in July 1994, three years after the unlawful ter-

mination. When commenting on the resolution of the case, Carnegie Mellon's dean of student affairs stated that "it's not appropriate that anybody be asked to declare a belief he doesn't hold. No one should be put in that position."

42. Marvel, "A Culture War," 1A.

43. Ray Bradbury, *Fahrenheit 451* (New York: Ballantine, 1979), 176.

44. Strossen, "Politically Correct Speech," 129.

45. Paul Richard, "Scrawling in the Margins," *Washington Post*, 5 March 1993, C1, C8.

46. Strossen, "Politically Correct Speech," 130–31.

47. See Alessandra Stanley, "Militants Back 'Queer,' Shoving 'Gay' the Way of 'Negro,'" *New York Times*, 6 April 1991, sec. 1, 23.

48. Mary Jordan, "College Repeals Speech Code," *Washington Post*, 12 September 1993, A1, A7.

49. "Polynesian P.C.," *Chronicles*, October 1993, 50.

50. Suzanna Sherry, "Speaking of Virtue: A Republican Approach to University Regulation of Hate Speech," 75 *Minnesota Law Review*, 933, 937 (1991), citing Matsuda, 2361–70.

51. See Strossen, "Regulating Racist Speech on Campus: A Modest Proposal" (hereinafter, "A Modest Proposal"), 1990 *Duke Law Journal* 559 (1990).

52. Ibid., 554 n. 358.

53. Ibid., 559.

54. Anderson, "Big Mouths," 60.

55. Hyde and Fishman, 1489.

56. For a discussion on the British experience with such problems, see Strossen, "A Modest Proposal," 555–60.

57. Hyde and Fishman, 1489.

58. Strossen, "A Modest Proposal," 560.

59. Strossen, "Politically Correct Speech," 132.

60. Hyde and Fishman, 1490.

61. See Anderson, 177.

62. Cf. Strossen, "A Modest Proposal," 535; Hyde and Fishman, 1486; Sedler, 651 n. 81. See generally Whitehead, *Religious Apartheid*.

63. Hyde and Fishman, 1484. See also Scott Gottlieb, "A Mockery of Justice on Campus" (hereinafter, "Mockery"), *Wall Street Journal*, 27 September 1993, A22.

64. Gottlieb, "Mockery."

65. Ibid.

66. See Hyde and Fishman, 1484.

67. Ibid., 1484–85.

68. Nat Hentoff, "Gregorian's Chant," *Washington Post*, 13 April 1991, A19.

69. Strossen, "Politically Correct Speech."

70. See "Speech and Reason at GMU," *Washington Post*, 13 September 1993, A20.

71. Ruchlak, "Civil Rights, Confederate Flags and Political Correctness: Free Speech and Race Relations on Campus," 66 *Tulane Law Review*, 1411, 1425, n. 60, quoting Presser, "The Politically Correct Law School: Where It's Right to Be Left," *American Bar Association Journal*, September 1991, 52–53.

72. Hyde and Fishman, 1472–73.

73. Ruchlak, 1428. See also William A. Henry, "Upside Down in the Groves of Academe," *Time*, 1 April 1991, 66.

74. Ruchlak, 1484.

75. *Smith v. Arkansas State Highway Employees Local 1315*, 441 U.S. 463, 464 (1979).

76. Id.

77. *Alexander v. U.S.*, 125 L. Ed. 2d 441, 452 (1993).

78. *Bantam Books Inc. v. Sullivan*, 372 U.S. 58, 70 (1963).

79. See *Pacific Gas and Electric Co. v. Public Utilities Commission of California*, 475 U.S. 1, 8 (1986).

80. *Thornhill v. Alabama*, 310 U.S. 88, 95 (1940).

81. Despite the important interests served by free speech, and the rather broad protection afforded by the First Amendment, free speech has never been viewed as an absolute right under the Constitution.

    Certain speech may be restricted, and some forms of speech, such as defamation, obscenity, and fighting words, receive no protection under the First Amendment.

    Subversive speech and speech intended to elicit illegal behavior may be limited.

    Speech regarding illegal actions may be prohibited when it takes a form likely to produce an imminent lawless act, although courts very rarely find that such circumstances exist.

82. 120 L. Ed. 2d 305, 315 (1992).

83. Id.

84. 124 L. Ed. 2d 436, 447 (1993).

85. See Anderson, 180–81; Sedler, 650–51; Strossen, "A Modest Proposal," 502–03. The Supreme Court has alluded that freedom of expression should have heightened protection within the academic environment: *Sweezy v. New Hampshire*, 354 U.S. 234 (1957); *Keyishian v. Board of Regents*, 385 U.S. 589 (1967).

    > To impose any strait jacket upon the intellectual leaders in our colleges and universities would imperil the future of our Nation. . . . Teachers and students must always remain free to inquire, to study and to evaluate, to gain new maturity and understanding; otherwise civilization will stagnate and die.

    Sweezy, 354 U.S. at 250.

86. Id. quoting *United States v. Associated Press*, 52 F. Supp. at 362, 272 (1993).

87. For example, in *Tinker v. Des Moines Indep. Community School District*, 393 U.S. 503 (1969), the Supreme Court upheld the students' right to wear black armbands in class to show their objection to the Vietnam War. In *Healy v. James*, 408 U.S. 169 (1972), the Court ruled unconstitutional the refusal by the university to grant official recognition to a student group (Students for a Democratic Society) on the grounds that the college disagreed with the group's philosophy.

   However, the Supreme Court has permitted some restrictions on free speech if the restraints are regulating the time, place, or manner of the speech. Further, restraints may be permissible if there is a material disruption to the educational process. See Anderson, 183.

88. Anderson, 184–86; Sedler, 650.

89. *Texas v. Johnson*, 491 U.S. 397 (1989).

90. Id. at 414.

91. *Cohen v. California*, 403 U.S. 15, 25 (1971).

92. *Collin v. Smith*, 578 F.2d 1197 (7th Cir. 1978), *cert. denied*, 439 U.S. 916 (1978).

93. *Operation Rescue v. Women's Health Center, Inc.*, 626 So. 2d 664 (Fla. 1993).

94. Florida Circuit Court Amended Permanent Injunction, Facts section (hereinafter, F.C.C. Facts), Par. D. See also F.C.C. Facts, Par. E. The injunction is reprinted as an appendix to *Operation Rescue*, 626 So. 2d at 677.

95. Cars entering the parking lot of the facility "sometimes [had] to momentarily hesitate or stop until persons in the driveway moved out of the way." F.C.C. Facts, Par. A.

96. Id.

97. "[I]n the instant case there is no indication in the record that women were actually prevented from obtaining abortions at the Aware Woman Center for Choice. The clash here is between an actual prohibition of speech and a potential hinderance to the free exercise of abortion rights." *Cheffer v. McGregor*, 6 F.3d 705, 711 (11th Cir. 1993) (footnote omitted).

98. Florida Circuit Court Amended Permanent Injunction, Conclusions section (hereinafter F.C.C. Concl.), Par. A.

99. See *Cheffer*, 6 F.3d at 711 (footnote omitted).

100. F.C.C. Facts at Par. I.

101. F.C.C. Facts at Par. B, C.

102. F.C.C. Facts at Par. D.

103. F.C.C. Concl. at Par. B.

104. F.C.C. Facts at Par. C, Amended Permanent Injunction Order of the Court, Parties section (hereinafter F.C.C. Order).

105. F.C.C. Order.

106. Florida Circuit Court Amended Permanent Injunction, Orders section, Par. 3.

107. *Cheffer*, 6 F. 3d at 711, 711 n. 11.

108. Id. at 712.

109. *Operation Rescue v. Women's Health Center*, 62 U.S.L.W. 4686 (30 June 1994).

110. As quoted by John Leo, "Not the Way to Stop Abortions," *U.S. News & World Report*, 29 March 1993, 17.

111. Ibid.

112. See, in general, Whitehead, *Religious Apartheid*.

113. See "While We're At It," *First Things*, August/September 1993, 73.

114. Richard A. Baer, Jr., "The High Court's 'S' Word," *Christianity Today*, 8 September 1989, 20 (emphasis in original).

115. Ibid.

116. Ibid., (emphasis in original).

117. Judith Bat-Ada (Reisman), "Freedom of Speech as Mythology, or 'Quill Pen and Parchment Thinking' in an Electronic Environment," 8 *New York University Review of Law and Social Change* 271, 272 (1978-1979).

118. Strossen, "A Modest Proposal," 567.

119. Aryeh Neier, *Defending My Enemy* (New York: Dutton, 1979), 4–5.

120. See Whitehead, *Religious Apartheid*.

121. See John W. Whitehead, *An American Dream* (Westchester, Ill.: Crossway Books, 1987).

122. As reported in "Abortion Bias Seeps Into News Media," *Citizen* (15 October 1990), 10.

123. Ibid.

124. Ibid., 11.

125. Ibid.

126. Ibid.

127. Ibid.

Moody Press, a ministry of Moody Bible
Institute, is designed for education,
evangelization, and edification.
If we may assist you in knowing more about
Christ and the Christian life, please write us
without obligation: Moody Press,
c/o MLM, Chicago, Illinois 60610.